THE THREEFOLD NATURE OF
DESTINY LEARNING

By the same author:
Awakening the Will, Principles and Processes in Adult Learning
Practising Destiny, Principles and Processes in Adult Learning

THE THREEFOLD NATURE OF
DESTINY LEARNING

COENRAAD VAN HOUTEN

TEMPLE LODGE

Translated by Karen Schnebel and Barbara Konig

Temple Lodge Publishing
Hillside House, The Square
Forest Row, RH18 5ES

www.templelodge.com

Published by Temple Lodge in association with New Adult Learning Movement 2004

Originally published in German under the title *Der dreigliedrige Weg des Schicksalslernens* by Verlag Freies Geistesleben, Stuttgart 2003

© Coenraad van Houten 2003
This translation © Temple Lodge Publishing 2004

The moral right of the author has been asserted under the Copyright, Designs and Patents Act, 1988

All rights reserved. No part of this publication may be reproduced, stored in a retrieval system, or transmitted, in any form or by any means, electronic, mechanical, photocopying or otherwise, without the prior permission of the publishers

A catalogue record for this book is available from the British Library

ISBN 1 902636 58 9

Cover by Andrew Morgan featuring a photograph by Wolfgang Schmidt
Typeset by DP Photosetting, Aylesbury, Bucks.
Printed and bound by Cromwell Press Limited, Trowbridge, Wilts.

Contents

Preface	1
Overview of the Learning Processes	3
Step V of Destiny Learning (Looping I)	4
Step VI of Destiny Learning (Looping II)	4
Step VII of Destiny Learning (Looping III)	5
The Threefold Nature of Destiny Learning	6
How does Destiny Learning appear in relation to 'new adult learning'?	8
Understanding Destiny (Learning Steps I–IV)	10
Transforming our Destiny (Learning Step V)	13
Exercises for Transforming the Double-beings (Learning Step V/Looping I)	16
Preparation	17
Looping I	18
Learning how to acknowledge and transform human relationships (Learning Step VI)	27
Exercises for transforming relationships (Looping II)	28
The transition from transforming to ordering destiny	42
Learning How to Order Destiny (Learning Step VII)	45
Practical hints for ordering destiny	46
Ordering karma—taking initiative (Looping III)	47

Summing Up the Threefold Work on Destiny 55

Appendix 1 for Educators 58

Appendix 2 for Educators 61

Appendix 3 for Educators: The basic gesture of speech as a means of transforming the Doubles—with reference to the four types of ether 66
by Enrica dal Zio

Preface

This supplement to the book *Practising Destiny* must start with a confession by the author.

Many people were inspired by reading the book to take the path of Destiny Learning—through seminars, individual talks and other ways—but the entire process could not be described. It gradually became evident that a good deal was missing. What were the reasons?

1. All adult learning demands that one goes through the whole learning process—since the seven learning processes are based on the seven life processes, which are a natural totality.

   In *Pracising Destiny* only Steps I to IV are described, along with some indications as to how Step V could be practised. The ideas that were put forward were incomplete from the point of view of the self-contained learning process of the adult.

2. The second reason was much more basic, and here follows my confession: I had assumed that if one has understood karmic laws in general and has practised them on one concrete example the rest would follow on its own. I was tempted by a kind of 'educator's optimism'.

   Although a lot was achieved, the 'transformation of destiny' and also the creative 'ordering of destiny' remained a problem.

3. With the many indications Rudolf Steiner gave last century between 1902 and 1924 it might have been easier at that time to transform old karma into new karma, but that happened very little. Today we are so hindered by the

conditioning of training systems and other illnesses of our culture that it is much more complicated to develop the ability to transform destiny. Many Double-beings appear that try to hinder this work, and many conflicts occur between people. Self-knowledge is a problem in itself but to transform oneself is a much bigger one.

Through the karma work of many participants in the 'new adult learning' a much more complete picture of the actual karma work came about. Out of that the so-called 'Supplement' was written, which contained new ways of learning and practising. It was written, however, only for assistants in karma work in order to try it out and improve it.

Many possibilities for new directions in education, in social communities, in psychotherapy and karma-diagnosis became apparent.

Thus many people have contributed to this book in order to compensate for the sin of omission by the author. I beg the reader to discern this through the lines!

At this time I want to declare my heartfelt gratitude to the many co-workers in Destiny Learning through whose activity this piece of work was made possible.

Overview of the Learning Processes

To clarify the terms used, the interrelation between the life processes, the Learning to Learn and the Destiny Learning is shown briefly:

Step	Life Process	Learning to Learn Process	Destiny Learning Process	
I	Breathing	Observing	Observing an event out of life, finding the gesture	Destiny Learning I
II	Warming	Relating	Placing single event in biography, finding the symptoms of the being	
III	Nourishing	Digesting, assimilating	Finding the karmic cause and learning task for this life	
IV	Secreting	Individualizing	Acceptance, saying yes to destiny	
V	Maintaining	Exercising, practising	Practising transformation of your Double	Destiny Learning II
VI	Growing	Growing faculties	Transforming relationships in the network of destiny	
VII	Reproducing	Creating something new	Ordering karma	Destiny Learning III

Steps V, VI and VII will now be shown and explained on their own. We call these learning processes Looping I, II, and III. Each proceeds in seven steps.

Step V of Destiny Learning (Looping I)
(Practising)

1. To do a 'freer' deed which is not influenced by the Double
2. Confrontation with the Double
3. Reaction of the Double
4. A further insight into the nature of the karmic cause
5. Find the learning task that arises out of this insight
6. Take that on and accept it
7. Search for the next 'freer' deed

Step VI of Destiny Learning (Looping II)
(Destiny relationships network)

1. Now that I have understood better the effect my Double has on other people, I can perceive the other's karmic situation with me. In order to find a 'freeing' deed in this respect, I ask myself 3 basic questions:
   - How do I understand the other's problem with me?
   - What did we create between us as a Double?
   - What 'freeing' deed can I do to lighten the other's problem with me?
2. Wait for what appears in the relationship and note changes in your own feelings or attitudes
3. Learning to read the reactions
4. What does this reveal about the karma between us?
5. The actual task between people will become apparent
6. Saying yes to the task
7. Search for the next freeing deed

Step VII of Destiny Learning (Looping III)
(Ordering karma)

1. Initiative—a 'free' deed. Either: make the necessity visible, take the initiative yourself
   or
   make the initiative possible
2. To study myself, my Double and all the relevant relationships that could be involved
3. To examine the life situation and the possibilities and impossibilities
4. Out of my old karma, does the initiative really belong to *me*?
5. Observe the social tasks involved
6. Accept the reality of what is possible or not yet possible
7. With new insights proceed to the next step

This book is therefore about the last three learning steps in Destiny Learning so that in the end the reader might have a deeper insight in the totality of the karmic learning process.

The Threefold Nature of Destiny Learning

Understanding destiny, transforming destiny, ordering destiny

We cannot overestimate the importance of the second learning path—'Learning from Destiny'. Here we are concerned not so much with general karma research, which reveals the endless, many-sided karmic threads that go through the history of incarnations, also with the many and important discoveries of what happens when the threshold to the higher worlds is crossed. Though both are important, they do not constitute the main issue here. The aim of the second, middle learning path is basically a renewed, transformed behaviour in the way we handle our daily human relationships. Thus Destiny Learning shows a way towards social renewal on the micro-social as well as macro-social level.

By 'learning path' we mean here a path whereby we learn through the experiences of daily life. It is a path that goes through an inner transformation towards self-knowledge in this respect. It is not a direct application of concepts, ideas or ideals about karma and reincarnation, nor is it a disciplined methodical prescription for the conduct of daily life.

This way shows itself as a social art that asks for original creative behaviour in each situation with our fellow beings. The path of Destiny Learning should school the faculties we need for this art of living.

Daily life itself will show the learning tasks. We often prefer to stay blind to this fact, and stay in the illusions in which we live. It becomes more and more clear in our time that every person has psychological problems—that modern biographies are proceeding from crisis to crisis. Depressions, delusions, unsolvable conflicts, hate, vengeance, etc. often derive from old karma that has neither been recognized nor transformed.

The main illness of our time is that we refuse to walk the path of Learning from our Destiny. This illness of our civilization is covered up by theories which promise successful recovery if correctly and generally applied. Or behaviour patterns are offered which if trained promise a practical solution. The path of Destiny Learning itself, however, is not taken into consideration. This would require the development of new faculties and capacities, an inner transformation in the central core of the person, to enable him/her to meet the demands of life in a creative way. Only then something new emerges that has future. Beautiful, often abstract theories or learned and trained behaviour patterns will only bring our culture further into disaster—because the living processes of reincarnation and karma are after all still the reality in which we live.

Destiny Learning—seen in this way—contains the key for a true Christian future for humanity in which the karmic ordering deeds we do for our fellow beings with whom we are karmically connected can have a healing value.

Destiny Learning thus taken through the complete process to the ordering deed shows a threefold gesture. This threefold gesture applied to the complete learning path showed as having a decisive influence, able to counteract the inadequate theoretical solutions indicated above.

When the Destiny Learning does not come to its full fruition—as the middle of the three learning paths—then 'new learning' also threatens to become a beautiful theory for generally solving the problems of our times and could harden into an empty methodology. This threefold process, which will be described further on, could protect us.

In the book *Practising Destiny* as far as I know nothing is mentioned that is basically wrong, but missing however, as mentioned above, are the two supplementary steps of 'transforming' karma and 'ordering' destiny as creative contributions towards the future.

How does Destiny Learning appear in relation to 'new adult learning'?

In the book *Practising Destiny* the first four steps of Destiny Learning were described with some indications as to how Step V could be practised. In the meantime many people have taken the indications seriously and discovered that, by practising, the karmic reality became more visible in its nature and more manageable in daily life. The path of self-knowledge was accelerated.

The new exercises for Steps V, VI and VII added many more insights and experiences. Therefore it was a necessary step to publish these new developments in Destiny Learning to make them accessible to everyone, for their own use.

As already mentioned, the most important discovery is the threefold gesture within the seven-step Destiny Learning path:

Steps I to IV leading to understanding destiny, connected to the basic human drive to know and understand.
Steps V–IV–III and again III–IV–V are a dynamic change process, bringing understanding into the transforming of destiny. This connects to our drive to develop.
Steps VI and VII, the third part, is the actual culmination of

the total learning process, realized in a re-ordering of our relationships and deeds. This connects to the drive to improve, meaning here the continuous striving to achieve the ideal human being.

(These three drives are extensively described in the book *Awakening the Will*.)

Please note that this threefoldness does not mean a fixed sequence but a living, ever-repeating and deepening path of self-knowledge.

To understand this, the way must be described methodically—and methodically means in this case a way that describes how new faculties can be developed at the same time.

In the following pages, the threefoldness of the learning path will be described in sequence.

Understanding Destiny

Learning Steps I to IV ⌐Destiny Learning I⌐

This process is described well enough in the book *Practising Destiny*. Therefore we will add only a few additional thoughts and highlight some open questions.

With the third step, 'Finding the cause and learning task', the question appeared again and again how these karmic causes can be discovered and verified by the teller of the event together with the group members.

Also the blockages were described in the book but not entirely completely and something more can be added.

When one asks a participant in this learning process how they come to the certainty that something one observes is karmically correct, one hears quite often: 'Through how a person talks and gestures while speaking.' When one enquires further with those people who can hear it in the speaking how this kind of listening really happens, they describe a special kind of feeling that can be distinguished clearly from other kinds of feeling. It is a self-evident feeling or a karmic sense of truth. It is often accompanied with a light vibration in the etheric body. This self-evident feeling does not show strong emotions, something sensational, nor stimulating elements. It is much more sensed out of the speaking itself. Also when one hears contributions of others, one can feel: 'That is not yet what it is'.

Only those who bring with them a certain clairvoyance or who have developed this already say, 'I see pictures'. These pictures also come as a result of dedicated listening to *how* something has been spoken.

Rudolf Steiner indicates that the karmic sensing faculty uses heart forces and is not an intellectual interpretation. It is important to be aware that this karmic sensing is latent in many people and can fairly quickly come to the surface, the more so when one practises it in a small group. However one must learn to distinguish clearly what comes out of one's soul as a reaction and what comes out of the observing-reading-feeling for the other. Distinguishing between these leads more and more to a certain kind of inner certainty. A karmic sense of truth arises alongside the normal cognitive feeling for truth. Important in the process is that the person who listens to the contributions from the group members does not close his eyes and look a long time in himself until some picture emerges, but listens such that an immediate response takes place. In the long run one learns to distinguish these feelings clearly from the endless varied perceptions from daily life. It is like a heart-centred listening-into.

In the beginning these reactions are still very global and vague, but particularly in the further step of transforming destiny they become more and more clear. In this first part of Destiny Learning the essence is to distinguish these perceptions from normal general reactions.

It remains a precondition that one is already to some degree an independent adult learner, as it is described in the first learning path (see *Awakening the Will*). We have to mention as well that the awakening of this new faculty is already being practised in the first phase of understanding karma, but the actual faculty of sensing destiny grows in the second phase where the transforming of destiny is being practised.

The result of the first four steps leads only to a first understanding of the laws of karma and a first understanding of the karmic forces that work in me and towards me. It should also be added that this way to understand destiny together with the exercises mentioned, if they are schooled regularly and earnestly, will lead step by step to a change of our value system, our judgements and our discernment.

Transforming our Destiny

Learning Step V ⌐Destiny Learning II⌐

Here begins the description of new processes not yet available in the book *Practising Destiny*. First will be described some general aspects of this 'transforming' process before the seven steps are outlined in detail.

1. Exercising, Maintaining, serves the search for truth, to learn the truth of one's own being in a meaningful way. The issue is to have the courage to perceive my unsolved karmic remnants and to accept them as belonging to me.

Another related issue is to understand our true karmic task as distinct from the so-called 'Doubles', which are behaviour patterns we develop that cover up or blot out our true karmic task. These Doubles may distract or stupefy to prevent us from seeing our karmic task, or they may lure us into illusions that imprison us. It is clear that the work on the first step of Understanding Destiny is a necessary precondition to acquiring the strength of courage and clear discernment required here.

This work needs to be permeated with a deep loving attitude, of loving the Doubles and karmic remnants. Only with acceptance of them as they are can they be transformed. One can regard them as opportunities offered to us which, just as diseases do, carry their healing in themselves. The karmic beings lead us to develop our true humanity and at the same time are healing forces between human beings. Truly every small exercise leads to sustaining our true humanity. Thus 'Maintaining' as a life process here means the sustaining of true humanity, which the Divine Beings have inaugurated in us.

2. When a karmic being that works in me has shown itself, it is asking to be transformed and accepted. Now the true transforming work can start in which the karma from the past and the preparation for the future is lifted into our consciousness.

Very much in me asks for transformation, metamorphosis, and development.

3. The aim is to be able to take on as a learning task the transformation of everything one can find in oneself as karmic untransformed and undigested remnants. Especially in this lifetime we have created so-called Doubles which are like a special category because they, as we shall see, reveal themselves as karmic disorder and escape beings. During the exercises in Learning Step V it will become more and more apparent what the real karmic task is and what the compulsive disorder being is that has placed itself as a resistance in front of the task. In doing the karma work we begin to see that for the present human being, under the present cultural circumstances and influences, the 'disorder of karma' has increased.

It was at the Council of Constantinople of AD 869 that the disorder of karma started and in recent times it has accelerated considerably. At that time it was the privilege of the Church to have a spiritual judgement and it was denied for the individual. Now today in almost every person there are compulsive complexes and behaviour patterns of many kinds that hinder and threaten our moral human development. It is therefore crucial that a learnable karmic path of self-knowledge as daily practice becomes part of adult education.

To simplify, we will call these disorder beings in the

following descriptions 'Double-beings'. The Double-beings have an intelligence of their own. They cover up our real karmic task, and therefore they take on a life of their own.

Although they can be differentiated into four different kinds according to how they appear and how they behave, they have nevertheless individualized traits. After all, we have created these beings ourselves as an 'event of avoidance'. They can appear as avoidance being, compensation being, cover up being, etc. In the moment in which we start to exercise with them to 'transform' them, they show immediately greater resistances. These resistances, however, lead to just those learning resistances that we need for the development of new faculties and abilities—which without these Double-beings could never be developed.

Exercises for Transforming the Double-beings

Learning Step V/Looping I   ⌈Destiny Learning II⌋

The life process at this stage is the Maintaining, which gives continuity to life. Through rhythmical exercising we can maintain and care for all learning processes. In the process of Destiny Learning the maintaining will be the continuous process of Destiny Learning bringing the connection between the last incarnation through this life today and towards the future and the next incarnation. One could say as well: the cosmic and the earthly biography will be connected. In earlier times religion provided this continuity. Since the human being became a 'head learner' he must take on this task himself. This can come about through continuous exercising. The transformation does not happen by doing the exercise once, but by repeating it again and again. This way of exercising should transform the karmic avoidance blockages (the Double-beings) who bring discontinuity, so that they will regain their task in the ongoing karmic development stream.

For overall understanding, it should be mentioned that the way consists of three basic exercises which can lead to transforming and ordering karma. Each of the three exercises consists of seven processes or steps (noted with Arabic numbers 1 to 7). The connection with the basic adult learning process will always be indicated with Roman numerals I to VII for each Learning Step.

Colleagues who have practised this exercise called these three main exercises the 'double salto mortale'. Then another term was used—the three different 'Loopings', for transforming and ordering karma. This term I will use in the text, because it is unusual and therefore easier to distinguish from other forms of exercises.

With 'transforming' we do not mean that this being will be forcefully destroyed, subdued or got rid of. Also it is not living out, reacting upon or sublimating. These do not lead to transformation. Even an outer change in behaviour does not lead to healing, although an adjustment to circumstances can be achieved.

Two preparatory exercises are now given. They are also described in the book *Practising Destiny*, so they are only indicated briefly here and are followed by the main exercise which will take us further.

Preparation

Exercise 1
Select a Double which you know well or you want to learn to know better. Preferably for first exercises it is better to take a small, simpler one that you can describe. For a number of evenings try to meet with it. For instance, place this being in front of yourself, observe it as accurately as possible and try to have a conversation with it.

Aim
This being should become objective, placing it outside oneself as if a neighbour, another personality, or like a friend. It is a first closer acquaintance whereby your fears should be overcome or your affection for it should be diminished. You can now describe the being.

Exercise 2
Examine the phenomena of this Double further by asking

questions such as: How does this being behave? When does it appear? Under which circumstances and how does it function in daily life?

When you have become acquainted with it in Exercise 1 above, you can also sense it in daytime as you more and more grasp the behaviour of this being.

If you cannot grasp it in the moment when it appears, you can still observe it in the daily review and recall how and in which way it has appeared.

These two exercises lead after some time to the possibility of performing an act that is not entirely under the compulsory power of the Double.

Step by step now the main exercise (see Looping I) starts that contains seven different activities which, certainly in the beginning, have to be executed as precisely and methodically as possible.

These seven steps will be first briefly described and shown in a summarizing picture, and then they will be described more extensively.

Looping I

Main exercise for transforming karma
Learning Steps V–IV–III and III–IV–V
This exercise combines two movements: one going towards the past after one has done a 'freer' deed, and one that goes towards the future to plan the next deed.

Thus the human being places himself in freedom in his destiny development stream.

The seven steps:
1. Doing a deed that is not influenced too much by the

Exercises for Transforming the Double-beings

Double but nevertheless has to do with the way it functions. It's called a 'freer' deed—freer than what one would do normally under the influence of the Double. It can be done in thoughts, in feelings or an actual outer act.

2. Now you confront this Double-being with which you are familiar, and show him the deed you have done. You do this by putting this Double outside yourself, face it, and observe it with great attentiveness and empathy. It is as a confrontation between the 'freer' deed and the Double.
3. Observe with great attentiveness how the Double reacts. Every little gesture, or mood, or thoughts that appear are important now.
4. What kind of indication does the reaction of the Double give to you in view of the karmic cause that you already have discovered in the first four Learning Steps (Destiny Learning I)? Through the nuances or qualities of its reaction, the karmic origin can be more clear, adjusted, corrected or shows as not yet complete.
5. Now one examines what this really means for the karmic learning task that lies before us in our present life. Thus one turns towards the future.
6. The discrepancy between the Double as avoidance being and the actual karmic task becomes more and more visible. This connection must be accepted anew. It belongs to you!
7. In view of the experiences that you had so far and the main acts you did in the activities in steps 5 and 6, you can now carefully plan the next freer deed.

Diagram 1. Looping I: Transforming the Double

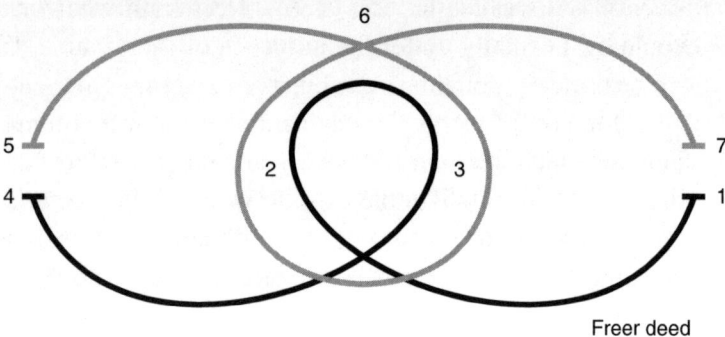

1. To do a freer deed, which is not influenced by the Double.
2. Confronting the Double with my deed
3. Reaction of the Double
4. A further insight into the nature of the karmic cause
5. Find the learning task that arises out of this insight
6. Take that on and accept it
7. Search for the next freer deed

This short description can be deepened and extended—in accordance with the experiences one has in repeating the exercise.

It is a dynamic process which develops in seven precise inner acts clearly to be distinguished from each other. It is urgently recommended to do each of the seven steps one after the other, because they build on each other and thereby the objectivity of each step is enhanced—while false interpretations are prevented.

The whole exercise should be repeated rhythmically and thereby will show a development. The transformation of the Double into new faculties takes place so that the new faculties bring you closer and closer to the actual karmic task.

Also the karmic disorder beings will eventually serve the actual karmic ordering deeds. The heart of the karma work begins to beat as daily destiny practice.

Practising the seven acts:
1. To carry out a freer deed.
In the beginning small steps are recommended, slightly loosened from bondage to the Double, which means an act that is not determined by or under the influence of the Double. The space for freedom of choice slowly increases and we are more able to act independently, free of the Double's control. The freer deed can be done in thoughts, for instance a basic conviction being transformed in our thinking; or in our basic feelings, such as a hatred or prejudice being changed; or in our will as an intention or decision about a deed we may want to do, such as writing a letter or planning a conversation. This is not just the opposite of our usual pattern, which is still determined by the Double. Know it well enough to make a slight change, which might catch it by surprise!
For Doubles with strong addiction features—spiritual as well as physical—we have to take care that forceful suppression, as well as sublimating, replacing, diverting or distracting, are not really 'freer' deeds. The individual ego should be appealed to as strongly as possible.
One should take into account that the human being is educated and developed through reincarnation and karma. Only through this can we become ever more free beings. When rhythmically repeating this looping exercise the exercise itself becomes more meaningful. As the karmic work proceeds to Steps VI and VII, the deeds of ordering karma arise quite naturally.
2. To confront the Double with the deed.
Through the first step you detach yourself from the Double.

With the second you turn towards it and confront it with your deed. Step 2 shows the effect, which your Double reveals and which has in itself already a freeing effect. One has to observe this very carefully.

For this you must be able to place the Double before you objectively. Something that lived in you stands now in front of you. Our force of 'uprightness', in a spiritual sense, is called for, to hold our stance and face the Double-being. At first this is difficult but it improves through rhythmically repeating the exercise.

Rhythm replaces strength! This applies to all the seven acts we are practising here.

3. Become aware of the reaction of the Double.

Step 3 consists of its actual reaction to the confrontation. There can easily happen a bewilderment between the observation and the interpretation, because the Double-being is still very closely connected with us and a kind of 'short circuit' can happen. To prevent this, step 2 has to be done first, which asks us to take distance and look at the Double with the greatest attentiveness, out of an ego-penetrated force of uprightness. (See Appendix 2.) Only if one tries to do this in full consciousness can one notice the reaction of the Double. Try to observe and perceive the phenomena, but do not use psychological interpretation or confuse it with our own subjectivity.

We must be aware that we created this being ourselves, that in the course of time it took on a life of its own. It has taken in many elemental beings and developed an intelligence of its own to live itself out, nourish itself, etc. *It even knows what it wants to prevent.* And now we defy it and do an independent act. Then it must react and make visible its position! Now we have to observe accurately what happens. Certain feelings can come up; often unusual unexpected thoughts emerge, from accusation or blame to high praise. Infinitely different reactions can show. When we observe meticulously, it will always react. With the interpretation of the reactions, however, we have to be very careful, because such beings are very intelligent and could conjure up many delusions. We could imagine much that is actually coming from us and not from the Double.

The sense of truth and ability to distinguish must be maintained at all costs. In the beginning it is best to leave the reaction without interpretation, just as an observed phenomena, and take it along to the next step. Also very helpful is to keep a record with short notes of the reaction. For instance, today he was friendly, now he is defensive, now he makes intelligent arguments, now he looks very different, or I experience him to be much stronger than I thought, or it shows a very different character trait, and so on.

4. From the present life back to the last incarnation.

This step demands an inner shift into the time, circumstances and culture in which one was in past lives. What we have discovered from the reactions of the Double in that last step throws a new light on the karmic causes from the past. The reactions of the Double and the concrete karmic causes start to show a specific correlation. Many people have a tendency to skip this step because they have already discovered enough about the present Double; but then we run the risk that the difference between this disorder being (the Double) and the actual karmic task in this life cannot be properly distinguished. Without a correct diagnosis there cannot be a correct remedy.

The transition from step 3 'reaction' to step 4 'karmic cause' in the last incarnation is a very big step and often needs an interval of sleep as support. Often learning from the night will be of great help for deepening the cause by putting the question to the night. The Double's 'reaction' throws light on the consistency of the 'karmic cause', which often breaks through as a new insight the next morning. It is astonishing how many new points of view about our old karma can emerge. The understanding of our destiny will grow wider and be considerably deepened, and more so when repeating the exercise.

Another support here is to have a picture of the many different kinds of karmic disorders that have an influence on us through our present culture.

5. Now we start looking to the future.

The deepening of the understanding of the past gives us the possibility to look forward. Indeed we look to our pre-birth intentions that were determined between the last death and the present birth, under the guidance of the Hierarchies. The midnight hour as the will to incarnate, the direction of thought in the Saturn phase, yes the whole preparation for the present life contains the real karmic task. But through the pressure of life and our biographical circumstances, the task is blotted out, distorted by the disorder beings and forgotten. Through the previous four steps we can now discover more about the true karmic task and learning possibilities that lie before us. The Double will have to be transformed and lessons learned before the greater life task can be realized.

6. The deeper understanding of the karmic cause, the renewed grasp of our present karmic task, to accept this, individualize it and take it on.

This is also an act in which the discrepancy between the influence of the Double and the actual karmic development task becomes more visible. In many cases one can experience today how strong the urge is to relive the situations of old incarnations, especially if one had worldly or spiritual leadership tasks and the present incarnation situation, as consequence, shows the opposite. The strong striving to repeat the last incarnation comes about, and our Double creates the possibility for it.

Saying yes entails therefore the acceptance of the difference between the disorder being and the real task. This discrepancy can create the motivation for the new, more free deeds in the next round.

7. Planning of the next freer deed—built on the six previous steps.

We should not forget that it should be a rhythmic process, not too big and not too small steps but realistic ones. The expression 'freer' deeds is used because our aim is to transform these Double-beings. Mainly they show a compulsory disposition which means that realistically it can take a long time. It is even possible that a total transformation cannot happen in one life, but that my own ego learns to handle it in a way that it does less damage to my fellow beings. Experience shows that much energy, which was invested in or consumed by the Double, gradually comes free and then is available for daily life and for the next Learning Steps VI and VII. The motivation for transformation grows through this process. It is important that this preparation takes place so that the next deed with which we start the next round does not fall back in some sort of reaction. How we prepare cannot be described here because it must be done differently every time, freely created and building further on the individualization that has just happened.

Further remarks for the handling of Looping I

Experience teaches us that in the beginning this exercise is a bit bothersome to do accurately and disciplined, but also that fairly quickly one becomes accustomed to it. Soon it becomes a living process, and in the long run a lifestyle. This exercise becomes then useful for any psychological disturbance. In Encounter Conversation Therapy it is already being used in individual counselling as a method, under guidance of the helper. It can be expected that a special form of psychotherapy will one day follow. As a lifestyle it becomes a self-recognizing self-development that can make a considerable contribution to the healing of every human soul.

An important support can be to keep records of what has changed at every step in each of the seven activities. The rereading of these notes often produces unexpected new insights. This is ever so important because karmic impressions in the beginning are fleeting and can be forgotten quickly. Best is to take half a page for each of the seven steps, number them and note shortly what was found in every step.

Before each new step one should pause to avoid false interpretations by jumping ahead too fast.

The rereading of the total process makes us aware of its dynamics. Meditating the above given form regularly or working in an artistic way strengthens it, and the inner relationship between the seven steps can be experienced more and more.

A very important experience is that by exercising the transformation of the Double in this way, overcoming the resistance of it, leads to a new spiritual faculty. Our weaknesses will become our future strengths—if worked at in the right way. This faculty expresses itself in an *increasing perception of karma forces*. We can already notice this through the increasing speed with which this dynamic rhythmical exercise can take place.

At some point we become conscious not only of our own karma but also our karmic relations with other people. A kind of network becomes visible with all the people we are connected with. Our sense of destiny awakens.

Through the ever-increasing freer deeds towards our Double, the veil is slowly lifted that has covered the karmic origin from our consciousness. It is as a lightening up of the karmic truth. Our past horizon is enlarged.

The seven steps, each for itself, should bring about a change in our learning process, to transform our destiny.

They will become in the long run a self-knowing and self-guiding way of life. The Double-beings provide the resistance which makes a conscious learning process possible.

A concrete example
To transform a 'power' Double-being.
We mirror in our time the mighty spiritual forming forces of the Egyptian period of history. At that time the human being needed to become ripe for a more earthly directed existence. There were then positions of power—but as a result of the gods working through the leader and therefore accepted in social life. In our time we experience, mirroring this time, an increased ego-consciousness and a stronger consciousness of the material world. The ancient positions of power, such as being worshipped or followed, are no longer appropriate. Instead of fulfilling the karmic task to develop totally new leadership forces, we often fall into the power-powerlessness tension. The seven acts of Looping I can be then applied, leading to a transformation of the power-powerlessness Doubles and opening the way to a new karmically oriented style of leadership. In this we will also have to use the relationships Looping II as described below.

Now it is time to work on relationships with our fellow beings in which as we know the Double-beings are also present and consequential. After we have 'worked' on our Double-beings for a certain time, approaching the relationships will be possible.

Learning how to acknowledge and transform human relationships
Learning Step VI

Regular work on my Double—and there are usually several—will soon show that this does not only concern myself, but that many relationships with other human beings (who have a karmic history of their own) have a part in it. In our time these relationships are becoming existentially important for our psychological and spiritual development, and in our work where human relationships are becoming ever more difficult. There seems to be an increasing chaos of conflicts in the macro- as well as micro-social sphere, which apparently cannot be solved. We meet with abysmal accusations, hate and aggressive behaviour among individuals and groups, and even between nations and racial communities. What is amazing is the fact that these social phenomena have hardly ever been investigated as far as their karmic origins and tasks are concerned—an approach that could initiate processes of karmic transformation. It is high time that healing social life by karma work should begin.

Exercises for transforming relationships (Looping II)

Up to this point our karma work has still been concerned with transforming our own destiny with our Double which has caused chaos in our lives. The exercises gave us a steadily increasing realization of karmic forces as a woven fabric or network, by which we are connected with our fellow human beings. In this, karma work shows a fundamentally social dimension. Rudolf Steiner therefore called it a 'network of love'. Karma work becomes work on human relations.

Our exercises go on in a similar way, but we are now concerned more with the influence our activity has on our fellow human beings—especially on the many karmic relationships that are linking us with each other.

The basic aim of transforming karma remains the same. The objective, however, is now an expansion of space. *Growth* is the life process that expands into the growing dimension of the realm of destiny.

As preparation, place on a large sheet of paper a karmic network of your life, noting names of persons who had a karmic influence on you. Who has been helping, restraining, hindering, or giving direction? This does not mean recording a biography of all one has suffered or experienced. No, a sense for destiny will help you envisage these facts in quite a different way. Only what is essential or karmically significant is considered. The network picture need not be complete to begin the exercise. It will already appear like a fabric woven of many threads. It has many colours, knots, conglomerations and holes; it is torn in some places and marvellously woven together in others. It is constantly moving.

It may be useful to observe the following areas when looking at your biography of relationships:

1. my spiritual path—important influences and meetings;
2. my personal friendships, love affairs and enmities;
3. lifelong relationships, family/heredity, deaths, marriages;
4. working relationships.

Now select *one* personal relationship and see whether this relationship has dissolved or come to an end or whether it somehow got stuck. Should I have acted in a different way but did not have the strength then to do so? Maybe I now have this strength because of my work on transforming my Double? Now you look more closely at this relationship.

Looking back on one's life there are many 'sins of omission'. There are neglected relationships or some that are unfinished. All are pleading to be taken up again if they have not yet been solved. Now you have to begin to practise with the same seven steps as in Looping I, but taking a new aim and proceeding in a slightly different way.

30 THE THREEFOLD NATURE OF DESTINY LEARNING

It is helpful to remember that transforming your Double by these exercises requires a certain amount of discrimination—and that it needs an ever more refined judgement of the situation when transforming relationships (Looping II). When trying to put karma in order as in the third main exercise, moral judgement is required at a very high level. What we called 'transforming relationships' actually calls for extremely complex and subtle processes, which have to change and adapt according to each different situation. Personal encounter requires a special social art. Each relatively free action creates a new situation because every time something is changed and given a new order in the karmic network.

Diagram 2 shows the processes and the questions they raise, and is followed by a description of the seven steps.

Diagram 2. Looping II: transforming relationships

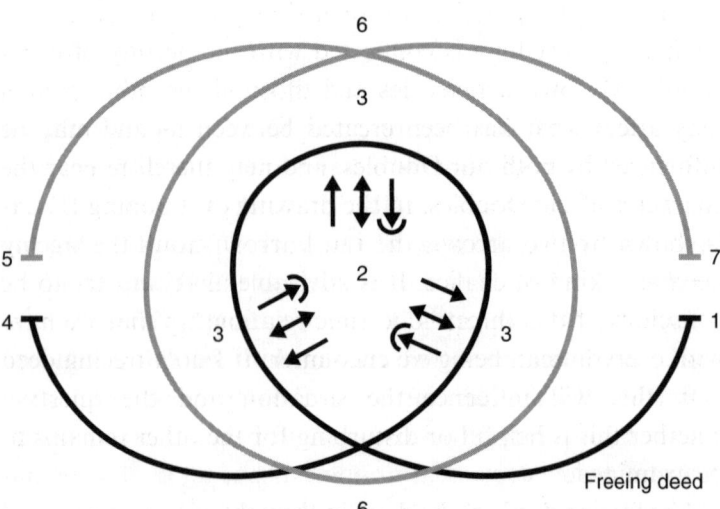

Exercises for Transforming the Double-beings

1. I look at the karmic situation of the other in as far as it is revealed to me, after I have come to a better understanding of the working of my Double on other people.
   a) I understand his/her problem with me.
   b) I can see the working of our Doubles on each other.
   c) Now I do one first 'freeing' deed.
2. I observe the other person and observe if our destiny changes. I observe changes in myself.
3. I read the reactions
4. What does this reveal about the karma between us?
5. What does this mean for my task?
6. Acknowledging the karmic task!
7. Preparing the next freeing deed.

This is a short description, which will be explained and deepened.

The relationships that are blocked and obstructed generally have to do with the destiny of several people. When beginning karma work it is better to start with one person at a time. Regular practice will then slowly reveal how and in what way everything is connected with the destiny of other people. My own deficiencies and those of the other person may affect what has been created between us and may be influenced by both our Doubles, and may therefore bear the character of the Doubles. In the drawing of 'Looping II' this is shown by two arrows; the third arrow shows the freeing deed as a kind of chalice. It is advisable always to try to be conscious of this threefold karmic relationship that we have with every human being we encounter. If I do a freeing deed now this will influence the situation and the question whether this is helpful or disturbing for the other remains to be examined.

The freeing deed can be done in thought only, in a changed

way of feeling, in transforming one's intentions, or in all three aspects. It often depends on circumstances whether one can really do anything that becomes visible.

It should be stressed here that work on a karmic relationship should be treated as purely individual learning and practice. We do not work directly with the other person, only individually and indirectly—although it happens quite often that the person concerned begins to sense something or to behave differently. In this way the freedom of the other person is guaranteed. The reason for this is that karmic processes take a special duration of time that differs for each individual. Therefore it cannot be brought about by collective decision whether 'the time is ripe' to see something of the Double or to find karmic causes. Looping II has therefore to be exercised individually and it is left to the free development of a person in how far it influences and affects the other as well as oneself.

There are no collective 'positionings' as in psychotherapy for special therapeutical situations. Karma work remains individual learning but the process allows mutual support and cooperation by others.

We are looking at a relationship in a threefold way—no longer in a way of confrontation but as a *karmic evaluation.* One could experience this like a positioning, putting oneself in the middle as step 2, and thereby becoming aware of the correlating links (see Diagram 2—Looping II).

Step 1:
One could think of the following three questions as an initial freeing activity for a relationship—if worked on with sincerity and dedication they tend to have this effect. The actual freeing deed then comes from the question: what could I do to free or relieve the other person from their problem with me?

Exercises for Transforming the Double-beings

a) What is the karmic situation of the other person? In what way do I obstruct or influence him by my Double which I have already acknowledged in Looping I ? Or, 'What ails you, under the influence of my Double?' The first part of the question points to the fundamental healing question that Parzival asks his ailing uncle Amfortas: 'What ails thee Uncle?'—meaning, 'What knot in your destiny are you struggling with?'

b) The second question concerns us and means: 'What ails us?' As a result of asking the first question, we can then ask what sort of obstructions have we created between us. This is a Double of relationships that is also known in modern psychotherapy.

c) As a result of the second question I can ask what has the other person not yet been able to transform because he/she did not have the strength to do so. This shows a basic line of approach out of an attitude of accepting the other person in the deepest sense in just the way he is. And this leads to the main question: 'What can I do to support him in his karmic task?'

Now the next steps of Looping II can be taken, and thereby a great deal will become apparent. It can often be recommended to repeat the three questions above throughout the looping process as they will always be seen in a different light.

If one regularly works on the first question (a) this will already bring about a complete change in judging the other person and, as a consequence, judging oneself. The relationship appears in a new light. Our social evaluation of certain situations is constantly changing. Fixed judgements are being revised.

The second question (b) throws new light on the generally accepted duality of judging as either guilty or innocent, right or wrong, good or bad. Instead something called 'ethical individualism'—as Rudolf Steiner calls it in his *Philosophy of Freedom*—should be evolved, which shows that each social situation is different from any other and demands a unique way of dealing with it. Generalizing and abstract truths would begin to die out as they do not fit the reality. 'Blame' is withdrawn where irrelevant. Our focus of attention may shift from justifying oneself to interest in the other.

The third question (c) brings to mind what social predicaments we have created for ourselves. They will keep us bound until we seriously devote ourselves to dealing with our karmic relationships, which is a realistic way leading to social healing. This would be an act that could also facilitate the karmic task of any other person involved. The healing of social life begins with a free inner or outer deed.

Step 2:
As in Loop I, you now observe the total situation—the Double of myself, of the other, and what has been created between us—in the light of your freeing deed. At first you may only be aware of changes in your thoughts, mood, feelings or attitude in yourself towards the other person. You may observe changes in how destiny presents the next new situation. Your environment begins to perceive you differently, as many people noticed after privately doing this Looping II.

Step 3:
Reactions can be perceived in myself and in the other person by the way in which he expresses himself to me. Thereby I may realize that something is loosened in me and that the connection or the relationship is changing. It is more difficult, however, to sense what is happening in the other person. I

myself have found that working with destiny sometimes brings about quite unexpected events, which show that something has started moving.

In this process you discover the virulence of what you are holding onto, or have been blind to in yourself or the other person. Perhaps they have been calling for your help and you did not ask the Parzival question. It requires some profound honesty and a quiet interval to allow these questions to mature and show their effect.. The main activity of Loop II is around the questioning 'What ails me?' and 'What ails thee?'

We should not forget that although apparently nothing happens, the other person can experience the spiritual effect during the night. And so very often quite unexpected encounters take place.

Step 4:
From these reactions particular aspects or indications of the original karmic situation during a previous life will appear. Through life experiences and social functions in past lives we learned and developed certain capacities or convictions which are present in us now as 'natural'. Therefore we are confronted here with how to really live this present life and not a rerun of the past and 'who I was then'. The other person may carry a subconscious karmic memory of the past situation, which is superimposed on the present and affects the relationship between you. In our time, past karmic memories are coming to the surface more and more; they challenge us to integrate rightly what we bring with us from the past and what we should be learning in this incarnation.

Very often connections through several incarnations become visible. This happens rarely at the beginning but will occur more often if freeing deeds are repeated regularly and sincerely. The night is a great help in this. One goes to sleep with the reactions of relationships and with the Parzival-question in mind. One awakes with a clearer understanding of what has happened because during sleep one has remembered one's karmic task. The meaning of life becomes clearer; disorder decreases.

Step 5:
In so far as relationships have to do with spiritual development and how we are one another's teachers and companions on the journey, a new understanding can emerge by assessing the learning opportunity to be found in the present situation. The blockages and resistances will become the future new faculties if we penetrate through and transform the phenomena, not avoid them. As a consequence the real karmic development task becomes clearer and points towards the next action which will still have to be accepted (6) and prepared (7).

Step 6:
Individualizing in step 6 shows something unexpected after some time. The reactions of our Double or the being that is hindering us will slowly but steadily change in character. They will become more and more our advisors, indicating the direction we have to take. The Double reluctantly becomes a kind of caring figure, showing what can be achieved and preparing for what cannot be achieved at this time. In anthroposophy he is called the 'Lesser Guardian' who awaits us in front of the threshold, pointing out our obstacles as well as showing us how to overcome them. That is why in step 2 my own self is positioned at the centre of Loop II, to observe human relations and to read their reactions.

Step 7:
Freeing deeds are prepared over a steadily expanding area. An important aspect in these freeing deeds is the act of forgiving.

Up to now we have been starting from individual, self-determined actions—not conflict management or solution by a group. In an obstructed relationship one can transform one's own part in the whole relationship by a consciousness that admits that we are all responsible and involved to a certain extent. This releases the others from their attachment and alleviates their destiny. What is going to happen with the karma of the others has to be left to the leading beings of our destiny. This is something with which we cannot interfere.

Looping II—and all that has to do with it—could be used in conflict solving but only as the work of an individual in his/her part in a conflict.

Further indications for Looping II
Until now we have shown that karma work has to do with our relationship with another person. For the initial exercises this is correct. In reality, however, human relationships will show interweaving threads that are connecting several persons. These ties will gradually become visible.

Also our relationship with deceased persons may appear. We have to consider that the dead are often working on their destiny and what attached them to us, so that our freeing deeds may be an act of liberation for them. The dead are often much closer and have a much stronger influence on us than is generally assumed, and karma work should involve them. I could often register reactions to freeing deeds from the dead; they even gave helping hints and assistance. If we find that deceased persons to whom we have been connected appear in the network, it is important to know that they are in a process of liberating themselves from their hereditary ties. The deceased may experience that we help them in their further development if we by our freeing deeds can loosen the ties that link them to these forces. They may also be able to help us in turn, depending on how far they have already been able to liberate themselves in their spiritual and soul life.

The whole situation may be influenced by a family angel working through heredity, or by a group of colleagues, or by some religious order. Even the spiritual being leading a work organization can exert a strong influence on the relationship between persons. We have to take into account that all social institutions are constituted under the influence of leading spiritual beings that can create their own Doubles, to which we are more or less connected as well. Karmic work is needed also in this area so that free deeds may undo ties with creativity according to the requirements of each different situation. Here the ordering element of karma work begins—especially as a preparation for Step VII, 'ordering my karma'.

The work done for one relationship can be now extended to several persons. Thereby a network becomes visible that can be transformed by our work. In order to point out the obstructions in a relationship it can be helpful to make a small mental graph of each situation as in step 2, and to see that the individual relationship to each person is quite different.

Looping II should be practised repeatedly until as a result the first outlines of a network—also with deceased persons—have been visualized and experienced clearly. Most people need practical help at first in order to practise Looping II. Only after this has been achieved to a certain extent can one begin Destiny Learning III.

When working on a relationship it is important to realize that conditions may of course be left the way they are, but they will have to be solved some time anyway. It is the clear

Exercises for Transforming the Double-beings

recognition of the situation that makes us free. Karmic forces that so far have not been detected can captivate us and determine our lives. To deny them means to have illusions about ourselves or to remain enslaved by our desires. The only way to overcome our weaknesses is to clearly acknowledge them. This is part of the process of maturing and it is the central aim of adult education: that my humanness is developing steadily; that I will be able to recognize what is happening in human encounters in relation to destiny, and be able to do transforming and ordering karmic deeds.

Many people have allowed their subconscious feelings of guilt to become a Double for them. Instead of transforming their previous mistakes so that something new can arise, people tie themselves to them in some sort of self-punishment. This can even be intensified if we are constantly exposed to the blame and derogatory judgement of others. Looping II should help to ask oneself a very simple question: 'Would I have been in a position to act differently at the time? I had no understanding for the particular situation and too little strength to do anything else then... But maybe I can find the strength now to go about it in a different way.'

In order to develop healthy forces of atonement instead of remaining caught up with feelings of guilt, it can be a help to look carefully at present or past situations and try to answer the following questions:

What have we received from others?
What do we still owe others?
What have we been given as a gift from the divine beings that have created us?
What do we owe them and the earth?

When asking these questions three types of obstructive Doubles may appear:

1. guilt—punishment—drugs or other addictions;
2. arrogance—feeling a special person, or the chosen one who is blind to the needs of others;
3. to see only the deficiencies—one's own or those of others (in both ways one is not free).

One has to create a balance—a balance between the gratitude for all that we have been given, and an acceptance of all our defects and all the sins of omission we have ever committed. Thereby our attitude of being basically bad or always good may change considerably.

Artistic support
In order to give support we put the seven steps together in a picture (see Loop drawing). One could meditate the process so that they can become a habit in life. It could be possible to recite them or to put them into movement in Eurythmy. A very effective support is to paint or model in clay to express in gestures each step in the process. Pastel drawing is a useful medium for this.

Artistic work can help in intensifying the transformation process and indeed has proved to be an essential accompaniment to the Destiny Learning exercises at every stage. It helps come into a sensing experiencing level that can reveal what head and words could not. It is important not to judge or interpret the results—the person's own process while doing the artistic activity is the main purpose. We are aware much more could be developed for doing this karma learning work via artistic means.

Some tips for educators and facilitators:
My own Double can be active when working with group members. It will help if my own forces of atonement have

been awakened, by doing this work on myself and with others. This can help to create a balance.

1. Watercolour painting in veiling technique could help develop forces of atonement.
2. Practising equanimity exercises helps to maintain health and this balance is also a force of atonement.
3. The basic idea is that we are all connected, 'for better or for worse'. To be a saint is an illness. To be a sinner is self-destruction. To develop forces of atonement is the Christian way of balancing; it is a healing force.
4. Try to learn the language of atonement. For this you should practise Looping II with a balancing, healing attitude.
5. As concerns the relationship between educator and participant, one should always keep in mind that Seminar I (Learning to Learn) has to be accompanied by the attitude of 'making the learning process possible'; Seminar II (Destiny Learning) by the attitude of a 'fellow being' that participates on the same level as the participant. He shows by his own examples how it can be done. In Seminar III (Spiritual Research Learning) when it comes to moral decisions, the attitude should be that of a 'companion or colleague' for the other person's spiritual path.

Social effects of Looping II
Example: Within one lifetime one can be a so-called 'egoist' as one does not know the conditions of one's life before birth or after death, or in previous incarnations. Only the present life is all-important! When working with karma the veil that conceals all this is lifted and one can realize that this egoism may as a consequence provoke a craving for power, reprisal or revenge.

The high value of forgiveness, the redeeming act of reconciliation, and many other attitude changes will become evident and can be experienced. Thereby new social values can develop. It is this work on human relations that can awaken and develop these new social virtues. Karma work on our relationships as in Looping II can therefore be a kind of healing work in the social field. The ego becomes creative in the social field and thereby contributes to the Ego of Humanity as a development for the future. Through continuous work on our social relations as in Looping II, a true kind of 'social art' can develop.

The transition from transforming to ordering destiny

When development is ready to move from Looping II towards Looping III the following features can be observed:

1. If regular growing and interweaving of the network of destiny takes place, supported by a growing capacity for karmic review, then what we may call our 'karmic horizon' expands.
2. Through the participation of the deceased a vertical expansion may result.
3. If karmic causes can be traced back over three or four incarnations there is an expansion in time.
4. If one realizes that certain events in a person's destiny seem to signal a preparation for future responsibilities, this means that there is a growing vision into the future—into the time stream from future to present.
5. One may begin to experience more clearly how the Christ-being accompanies our destiny in a kind of spiritual leadership.

Exercises for Transforming the Double-beings 43

This transition has to do with the aim of karma work. The main intention is to transform old unredeemed karma as a healing and redeeming process for the future. This intention is seldom totally fulfilled and is therefore carried on as an inner necessity in life.

The wish to *order* destiny derives from a different source. Almost every person has a profound and sometimes deeply hidden longing to be able to do something new and unique for the progress of mankind. He becomes conscious of this at some point in his life when he is confronted with the needs of his time. 'What does life demand that I should do?' may be his feeling—'What should I contribute?' or rather: 'In what way can I arrange my destiny so that I can serve the development of the world?'

Ordering destiny accordingly may mean giving direction or creating harmony. The main thing is that one experiences the question the world asks me. This question may arise out of a direct confrontation or experience in life or out of my interest in current events: 'What is needed, what should happen in this world now?'

New abilities and also fresh life forces have come up through working with Looping I and II. Should I use this only for myself or for my fellow human beings, for nature, for the earth, or for global aims? This is a truly moral question. People often describe this as a strong impulse to take on initiatives that have altruistic motives because those are directed towards more objective aims. There is always the possibility to leave it—these aims can also be pursued by others, there is not only me to do this work.

In this field the free deed becomes more and more important. Everything else has been like a preparation. A freer deed confronting my Double, a freeing deed for my fellow human beings and now a free deed for the world. For many people the real enlightenment and the full meaning of karma and reincarnation now becomes clear.

Thereby the next step (VII) is approached. In the life processes, that is the stage of *Reproduction*. Transformed into the highest aim of adult education this becomes a capacity for initiatives in order to perform deeds that will order destiny and contribute to the further development of mankind.

Learning How to Order Destiny

Learning Step VII ⌈Destiny Learning III⌋

Working on Step VI, which implies working on relations with our fellow human beings, brings about deep feelings. Actually our whole life is a process of meetings and encounters. There are encounters that have been caused by our past life functions and which are reappearing now in our biography, placed there by the wise guidance of this world. A successful encounter is a healing of karma. A failure will lead to a continuation of old karma. The network of the threads of destiny will therefore mean either imprisonment or a network of love. The powers ruling karma have created this as an opportunity for us; however, we often allow ourselves to feel more or less tied up and entangled in it instead of going our way freely. As we are discovering here, 'reproduction' does not mean to replay who we were in the past, or to repeat the same successes or mistakes, or simply improve on talents and skills. Karma is now future oriented.

It is hard to perform deeds that will put our destiny in order. So far we have been working on the transformation of our karmic past into the future and thereby developing a sense of karma. Now we should learn to perform deeds that would be good for as many fellow human beings as possible, i.e. that will affect the future. Now we shall have to deal with the consequences of deeds—no longer the transformation of past deeds or events. These deeds will have the character of *initiative*.

A moral sense for the consequences of karma-ordering deeds has to be schooled. Whenever we have done something, our impression—already the next day—may be either a liberated, free, warm, glad, heartfelt feeling or a dark, tight feeling of omission and incompleteness. We feel a new kind of conscience for what we owe to humanity, the earth and nature. We also register in our conscience what human rights demand and what wrongs are done to human beings. It will take time for this new conscience of mankind to individualize and to become a more personal conscience. Karma work will support this. It will appear as a kind of preview of the possible consequences of our decisions, initiatives or deeds. It can be called *karma preview*.

An ego that has awakened to the voice of conscience will be asking a different kind of question about what it means to be creative.

For the first time—as Christ has become the Lord of Karma—we are able to order our relations network in such a way that we can help carry another's old karma or take upon ourselves some portion of that karma. This means to cooperate in harmonizing the cosmic order of karma.

'*From our time onwards human beings have the chance to consciously work on the evolution of the earth utilizing the forces that bring order into karma because he (Christ) will be the Lord of Karma.*' (S. O. Prokofieff)

Practical hints for ordering destiny

a) Karma preview is a faculty already latent in us; it has to be awakened by karma work. We have also deep in us our prenatal intention of adding something new to the development of the earth and mankind (in freedom)—this should be activated in Step VII.

b) The deed should be done in such a way that it will

contribute to the good of as many other human beings as possible, in a way that supports their karma.
c) This should be done not as in the old chain-reaction of cause-and-effect in the sense of putting right old damage, but as a loving, healing deed. As a consequence the old chains fall away. For this it is necessary to create some sort of free space in which decisions can be taken. It can be practised in doing rather inconspicuous deeds in human relationships—like replying to offensive remarks in a benevolent, favourable and supportive way, or by not correcting a false statement but by pointing out something else that will indicate the truth. In the daily review in the evening one could try to reflect on how one might have reacted differently in human contacts in the sense of ordering destiny. It is also possible, in the daily review, to reflect on what you could have said, and write this down in a sentence for yourself, in order to become more aware for the next occasion.

In the deepest unconscious part of our souls there lies the life force of *new hope* which can be a decisive help in Steps VI and VII. We cannot know what our future will be like, but we can rely on a sort of natural confidence that there will always be a future. And we may have reason to hope that karma may accompany us and support us through all our future incarnations.

In order to learn how to creatively order our destiny, we can apply Looping III which follows more or less naturally out of Looping II.

Ordering karma—taking initiative (Looping III)

This Loop exercise can be done before the decision to start the initiative, or as needed along the way as reorientation, or try

48 The Threefold Nature of Destiny Learning

it out with an initiative out of your past experience. The most important difference between Looping II and Looping III is that what was in the centre in Looping II now moves to the outside—to the periphery—and the individualizing, accepting step 6 is in the centre.

In the transition from Step VI to Step VII of the learning process the two circles have changed over. What has to do with the past goes to the periphery and what is concerned with the future is now of central interest. So ordering karma has become initiating deeds oriented towards the future—deeds that will serve our fellow human beings, the earth and the cosmos. They originate from an understanding for what the earth needs and the intention to serve those spiritual beings who have given us infinitely much and thereby enabled us to become human beings that can fulfill their mission in freedom in shaping the future.

Diagram 3. Looping III: ordering karma

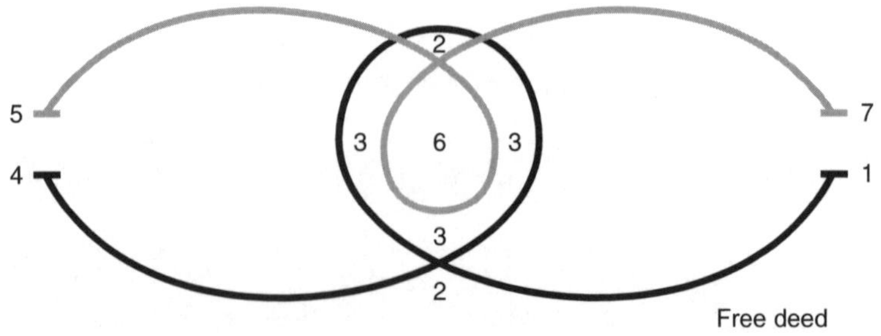

Free deed

1 Initiative—a free deed—either: make the necessary initiatives visible
take the initiative yourself
make the initiative possible
2 To investigate: myself—my Double and all relevant relationships in respect to the initiative
3 To examine: circumstances—possibilities—impossibilities
4 Cause: old karma becomes visible
In what way does this initiative belong to me?
5 To become aware of social tasks involved
6 Returning into the inner circle, individualizing, accepting, including the social environment. Accept reality of what is possible
7 With new insights—improve initiative and act on it!

Our self awareness and our positive as well as our not-yet-transformed karmic relationships stand between the circles of the past and the future, either supporting or obstructing our present initiative.

Step 1:
We are now asked to do a first step in spiritual research in order to find the right question that should be answered. The last creative Step VII on the path of learning from destiny is at the same time the beginning of a path of spiritual research. Two learning paths meet. One may also say that karma work leads us towards spiritual research. 'What does the world demand?'—and it means training the faculties that we need in order to do real spiritual research.

In these steps one should not forget that even the so-called smallest deeds are of high value if executed in concrete, realistic and moral terms.

In this first step a free deed should be accomplished. Your motivation comes from the environment, you feel called by the need: 'What does the world expect me to do?' The answer is at first an idea, to be followed by a decision. We should not neglect the many possibilities of free deeds. In taking initiative there are already three possibilities: to take it on oneself; to enable others to start an initiative; or (by intense spiritual research) to show and make people understand what are the true necessities and questions.

Step 2:
In steps 2 and 3 we try to honestly assess the initiative on as many levels as possible—for oneself, for others who may be involved, and for the initiative idea itself. Many questions can be asked in this context. For instance:

- I am investing my capacities into this initiative but I also bring in my weaknesses and deficiencies. What consequences will this have?
  Every initiative is also carrying the Double of the founders!
- Who is going to support and contribute to the initiative and what will this look like in practice?

No one can say that he/she has already transformed the whole of his/her karmic past. The beings that work as our resistances are still there, although we may have recognized them and may be able to deal with them. Into every initiative we bring ourselves, and we can only hope that our friends will help and protect us so that this will not do any harm to the initiative. It is important to be always working on self-development, which gives a kind of spiritual protection in the work. In the periphery we find all the others that are in some way connected with the initiative. In this way a new kind of teamwork among colleagues could result from karma work.

In this stage previous work on our Doubles and on our relationships will bear fruit and will help us to envisage clearly any possible moral consequences of our intentions for the undertaking.

Because we are aware of the idea for ordering deeds there is already an awareness for possible consequences. And we bring in all our own possibilities and limitations. By regular working with the help of Looping II a lot could be found out in this respect. All this will have to be looked at in detail with respect to possible deeds in the future. Thereby the karmic past is seen in a new light. It can happen that the past as a whole is a clear indication and preparation for what will have to be done at the moment.

Step 3:
One lives with the new idea of the initiative and examines very conscientiously any possible consequences that may come up in the future. This process may develop in completely different ways according to the character of the social environment of the initiative. Again many questions may be asked:

- Is the initiative the right one at a given moment—does it serve the environment or does it only serve me?
- What impact has the initiative on the social surroundings?
- Is it the right time as concerns sufficient spiritual preparation?
- What are the practical and material requirements?
- What will happen if this initiative cannot be realized—if I should withdraw or hold back?

There are many more questions that arise from one's own karmic situation and its hidden underlying questions.

If every initiative would make such a karmic-social diagnosis—and this could certainly be done by a group too—

many would not be started at all or would be taken up in a completely different manner.

Step 4:
In the fourth step, karmic review, we ask the question whether the karmic development—quite often over several incarnations—shows that this undertaking is really part of my own task and whether the time is appropriate. In this one should not forget that many new institutions have originated out of an intention formed in the midnight hour between death and rebirth. This is why our own biography may give us a clue. Illusions can arise on the other hand if the impulse is out of longings or wishes from an unfinished past.

This shows in a new context if we begin to understand the presence of the Christ-being as a guide who has appeared in the etheric world during the last century. This mission of a guide is also one of giving direction. Since the Christ knows and has accepted all our past karma, he carries and supports it with us, and guides us on the path of becoming ever freer human beings. Although working in the etheric world, he is at the same time affecting the etheric body of each human being.

He also knows our deeds and their consequences for our fellow human beings and the earth. He embraces the whole network of love that interlinks mankind, supporting and moving it in the etheric world which encircles the earth and penetrates our etheric body, and this is where we may transform the seven life-processes into processes of learning from destiny. Therefore we may in the end be able to form initiatives that can order karma and that may be in harmony with the aims of mankind.

Step 5:
Initiative always has to do with initiation and our

development towards our true potential. Many trials, tests and challenges will be encountered on the way. The ego today is given the space to choose, out of conscience and capacities, to become creative. This step means to identify the real task, and in what way the ego should commit itself.

Step 6:
The decision now faces us, along with recognizing what is at this time possible. What part of the ideal can be realized? Are we too soon or too late? What is the reality of the initiative? What life forces can I give to it?

Acceptance of karma as a task for the future is what we have to learn in this step. On the one hand we may remember our midnight hour between death and a new birth when we received the impulse, on the other hand we see that the realization of this impulse on earth is made possible by the way in which Christ is guiding our destiny.

Now it becomes clear why this step, which in the background has to do with individualizing one's own destiny, is so central in this Looping: it is the main experience in all learning processes!

The physical and psychological health of every human being depends on whether he can find and work on the initiatives that belong to him.

Step 7:
After our commitment has been made, the spiritual beings behind the impulse can confirm, strengthen or correct, according to its spiritual validity and credibility. The initiative can be planned and prepared much better if we can rely on discoveries made in the previous steps.

In summary:
It is good to experience Looping III as a whole and to follow the movement of its different steps. Only then one can see the first three steps (1, 2 and 3) as a kind of preparation for the initiative. One grasps the idea and links it to the persons with whom one feels connected or who may be concerned; everything is related to one's own ego and that of the other participants (2 and 3).

Then everything is linked to the last three incarnations (4), whereby it becomes possible to see a relationship between these developments and the present initiative, which in itself leads to the future.

We may have a glimpse of our real task in step 5 and it can individualize.

In step 6 the whole is looked at in a kind of overview.

Step 7 may then lead to further planning and preparing the initiative.

When this process is taken up and repeated at regular rhythmic intervals it can accompany the initiative and strengthen it considerably. In this way our destiny is integrated in the development of mankind and the world.

Summing Up the Threefold Work on Destiny

We hope our attentive reader will have realized that the threefold path of learning from destiny is to be considered an organic whole by the person who is learning. We have so far characterized the three levels of 'understanding destiny', 'transforming destiny' and 'ordering destiny'. Thereby we have shown that each part has its own aims although one level is based on the other. Also one level depends on the other, because unless karma is fully understood it cannot be transformed, and individual karma has to be transformed—at least partly—before it can serve in the evolution of mankind and the earth.

This fact will become even clearer if we consider who or what these three Loopings serve:

Looping I serves one's own development—a steady process of transforming one's own (chaos-causing) Double.

Looping II serves our social development—steadily transforming human relationships with the great aim of carrying and supporting the karmic network of love. This means a free individual work for a new karmic community which may lead very far—as far as towards helping to carry the karma of mankind.

Looping III is training the faculties that are required in order to be able to contribute to the evolution of mankind, the earth and the world as a whole. This creates the preconditions for the next step in learning creative spiritual research work.

This implies that one is in a position to take on initiatives, to realize and to carry them in order to answer the needs and demands of the world.

The three times seven practising processes—Looping I, II

and III—also show a threefold path which can make us more free as a human being—and this is the aim of learning from destiny.

One should not forget that this threefold karma work, as described here, is part of the whole new concept of adult education. Acquiring self-knowledge is basic to becoming a more responsible human being—but the previous path of learning was concerned with self-reliance in adult learning, whereas the following deals with creative research learning. All these paths of learning are carried on through seven fields of study which are part of and naturally supported by many practical exercises and concepts.

The new concept of adult learning is one whole subject which cannot be practised in parts or special details. An example can clarify this, and in this we refer to what has been said about the new language of destiny in *Practising Destiny*.

Why is karma work of vital importance for every human being?

Karma work will lead to the conviction that what seems to be impossible physically is possible spiritually. Practising karma gives this conviction a reality in life, it gives basic confidence to our 'hope' for meaning in life—for meaning in humanity—and a meaning and aim in the evolution of mankind. The power of faith gives us the conviction that this is so, the power of hope gives us confidence. But unless both these are nurtured by the power of love, which is at the depth of the soul, all this is but a pious dream.

Why should one practise karma work? Because mankind badly needs this since entering the twenty-first century.

In a survey showing the seven fields of study for the educator, the capacity for encounter is depicted on the left-hand side with the three ways of learning on the opposite right (see: *Practising Destiny*). What would happen if the faculty for encounter gave wings to karma work, and if on the other hand karma work influenced and nurtured human encounter more and more?

In human encounter destiny always plays a part, albeit mostly unconscious. If through karma work people became conscious of this fact, a new way of speaking and a new way of listening would develop. The capacity for encounter meets learning from destiny. In the middle of the seven fields of study there is the 'word'—the new language of destiny. This happens through the new way of encounter on the one hand and through the threefold karma work on the other. The path of learning and the faculty for encounter complement each other. This can really serve as a leading image in every conversation and in every 'encounter conversation therapy'.

Appendix 1 for Educators

The life forces of the soul:
new faith—new love—new hope

These three life forces have been referred to in the previous text and therefore require a more detailed description.

For the educator who sees his task in teaching karma work the following is especially important. In the subconscious part of our soul there are three life forces that are deeply connected with the core of our soul. These are the powers of faith, love and hope.

These three life forces that are working in the subconscious part of our soul constitute the bridge between the seven life processes and our ego, which is learning day by day. They should therefore be constantly called upon and activated when doing karma work.

What we call the new faith is dealt with mainly in the Learning Steps I to IV, as discussed in 'Destiny Learning I'. New faith in this context means to know all that the understanding of karma brings. It is like feeling a certainty that the laws of karma make sense and have a deep meaning. But our sense of truth has to strictly rule out any speculations.

The power of love as a life force is of the utmost importance in Step V where the transformation of karma begins. How can the Doubles, the opponents and the forces making chaos be transformed unless they are acknowledged and even loved? By the way, our etheric body gives us the power of metamorphosis, of transforming and also the powers of healing. The educator will have to find a way to constantly arouse these powers of love as life forces in the process of transforming karma.

In the end the powers of hope are referred to mainly as giving confidence for the future as in Steps VI and VII, because in this we shall always have to do freer deeds that have consequences for our fellow human beings, the earth and the evolution of mankind. In this one also has access to the new faculties of natural clairvoyance. Step VI (karmic review) and Step VII (karmic preview) also have to do with new forces of love and hope.

The educator has to understand that if he is cultivating these three forces during his work with his fellow beings this will have a healthy effect on the participants. The power of faith will work on our soul, the power of love on our etheric organism and the power of hope on our physical body.

They will have to be applied and practised in a rhythmical way whereby faith, love and hope as life forces of the soul will slowly be strengthened—as in the seven exercises in 'Destiny Learning II'.

Thereby life forces will come free out of the forces that have so far been preoccupied and will now be available to heal our astral, etheric and physical bodies with new faith, thanks to the benevolent forces of karma. The etheric body as the body that carries life can then be free to order karma in a less selfish and more loving way, so that it will heal. The deeds ordering karma—of which we can only hope that they will be good—are born in the soul as a kind of existential confidence which gives our physical body the strength it needs. In this way the process of transforming karma—as in Step V—may become a liberating, healing and strengthening path that will make it possible to re-order karma. The life forces of the soul—new faith, new love and new hope—can then be at the disposal of Learning Steps VI and VII, which all involve freer deeds and tend towards achieving the aim of all karma work.

Summing up one could say: in the subconscious realm of our soul the Ego rests as our force of faith, lives as our force of love, and *is* our force of hope.

Appendix 2 for Educators

The three exercises for schooling of ego forces: attentiveness, devotion, uprightness

The educator will have to live with the question how it is possible to transform life processes—the seven different ones—into conscious adult learning. We also know that every form of consciousness destroys our living vital forces. In the first learning process (see *Awakening the Will*) we can still become aware of it empirically. When we do this with sufficient attentiveness, the necessary interest and enough devotion—in which one never gives up inner balance as an independent learning person—it shows that this leads to an individualization of all learning processes. Here the human being learns, changes, develops itself and finally comes to a realization of himself. It is however much more difficult to understand when this relates to Destiny Learning and concerns our self-knowledge, since also here the life processes must become death processes through our consciousness. Here also the living spiritual destiny forces, which work very strongly, must be transformed into conscious learning processes. For this process we have to acquire a deep understanding, and here we are led by the gift of attentiveness, the faculty of devotion, and the will of uprightness.

The adult educator must continuously school in him/herself therefore these three faculties so they are mastered. These are qualities with which one can recognize the adult educator. For this reason they are of great importance for all three learning paths, but especially for Destiny Learning.

Enhanced attentiveness becomes an awareness of how the

forces of destiny approach me from the outside. When directed towards the inside it will show me in which way I react inwardly. So we find a double attentiveness, like an increased consciousness that breaks through the outer and inner threshold. This should happen in all steps of learning.

Devotion is the opposite process. Our enhanced ego-activity sacrifices itself, entering into the karmic events, so that one can observe the essential moments by living into them. Thus we go from perceiving what has happened to experiencing it. This is a very big step which can only be taken if one does not only possess uprightness and balance but if one can hold to this constantly in both processes.

To be able to work with all three faculties at the same time creates the consciousness that is necessary for karma work. It will be necessary to initially practise one at a time and school it as intensely as possible. This type of 'new learning' should develop ever new exercises and didactic practices to develop this attentiveness for the inner and outer world. In attentiveness we are mainly working with our nerve-sense system.

At the same time devotion should be developed in many different exercises. This is mainly working with the rhythmic system, i.e. on the heart and the lungs. This also requires didactic practices. For karma work the central point here is that if the capacity of devotion is more strongly and deeply developed, one learns to hear the voice of karma in the way the other person speaks and articulates. One will also begin to speak the language of karma (for this see: *Practising Destiny*).

When practising both faculties regularly one will find that one complements the other, and that they therefore very much require and also develop the balancing power of uprightness.

It is important not to neglect the central process of learning, else one might easily be caught up either with the outward sense-observations or in strong inner experiences that are connected with our organs and our organism as a whole. Our research has shown that the power of uprightness will release both the complementary forces from their one-sidedness. It is the task of devotion to develop from experiencing things and events towards recognizing them.

When schooling uprightness we rely on the metabolic-limb system because the power of uprightness finds its physical expression in this part of our organism. In this area 'new learning' gives many exercises—artistic as well as social. And balance can always be experienced as an expression of uprightness.

In a second phase the three ego activities should be practised one at a time by doing special exercises, so that they can be applied simultaneously. This brings about presence of mind. A kind of educational presence of mind can develop if the three forces work together in harmony. Attentiveness is a new quality of the consciousness soul, which can be achieved by effort. The opposite, devotion, if it lacks attentiveness leads to a kind of relapse—one disintegrates.

However, 'devotion' combined with 'attentiveness' is something new and unknown, which can be developed without the person losing him/herself in the process. This means a strong force of balance and uprightness is necessary in order to get a good grasp of the situation.

These remarks on the importance of these three may be sufficient in order to understand why in adult learning these three ego-forces play such a central role in transforming life processes into learning processes—and why therefore the training of these is an absolute necessity for educators as well as participants.

If we as adults look at the small child and his development with our attentiveness as well as devotion, we may easily discover that the small child already possesses the power of uprightness when developing from the toddler towards a walking, upright person. Even more amazing is the development of speech in this small being, which derives from deep and devoted imitation. And already when forming the very first sentences one can feel the presence of a thinking, discerning being. It is like a miracle that during the first three years of his life the small human being has already overtaken the animal world in his development. Others can explain why this is so. We have to direct our attention towards the learning process that takes place in adults. It seems quite clear that as an adult we have to reconquer the given forces of attentiveness, of devotion and uprightness by ourselves and through our own efforts. And this happens in the reverse order: we have to do it with an independent, enquiring and investigating attitude. It might be a help to study carefully the difference between what happens to the child almost like a gift or out of an instinct and what happens in the adult who has to undergo an independent, practising and fully conscious process in adult education.

One could sum this up as follows:

Out of attentiveness—of the child—derives the ability to cope with our present time.
Out of devotion—of the child—derives speaking and listening, the karmic link connecting with our personal environment.
Out of uprightness—of the child—derives a presence of mind for our fellow beings.

The child receives these three gifts of walking, speaking and thinking, which make it become a human being. The adult develops them in the reverse order: thinking that is free of the brain, speaking that is free of the body, and he finds the meaning in fulfilment of his destiny. In doing so he is strengthening his uprightness in every crisis that he encounters, and he comes to decisions that are more and more free from the body. He takes on the path of freedom—which is the aim of adult education.

Appendix 3 for Educators

The basic gesture of speech as a means for transforming the Doubles—with reference to the four types of ether

by Enrica dal Zio

There are already many artistic exercises to support transforming destiny. One of great importance is speech formation—as described in the following article.

If we speak of gesture we mean what man expresses in his movements and in his mimic ability. There are countries where the national soul is directed very much towards the outside world. This shows in strong and differentiated movements of the hands, the arms and all members of the body, as for instance in the Italian people.

When watching the gestures of a person we may learn a lot about his personality. We can also ask this question in the plant world—what, for instance, would be the gesture of a plant. And if we observe it carefully we may discover that the gesture of a plant can tell us a lot about its origin, its botanical family, its environment and the working of substances in it.

The gesture reveals to us something that is hidden behind appearances and has to do with the deep inner origins of beings.

In man we can have deeper insights into his being from his gestures but we can also detect the intimate constitution of his soul.

In the gesture lives the will-expression of the human being, permeated by feelings. The soul-spirit element is present as

a picture in the gesture. In so far as the soul-spirit element lets the feeling streams in the picture of the gesture, the human being reveals itself outwardly in the force of its will. We are dealing here with the human being becoming visible in the sense that its inner world is carried outwards. But the human being is capable of experiencing his self-mimicking, his gesture in the same way as he becomes aware of the facts and events of the outer world. In the awareness of the gesture is then a kind of fulfilment of our consciousness about the inner nature of the human being.
(Rudolf Steiner, *Sprachgestaltung und dramatische Kunst*, GA 282, Dornach 1981, p. 82.)

This ability of the human being to become aware of his own gesture is the background for any kind of healing in the work on gesture as well as speech formation.

In a lecture published under the title *Overcoming Nervousness* Rudolf Steiner tells us that it is good 'that man tries to watch himself in the way he walks, how he moves his hand, his head, how he laughs, etc., in short if he tries to visibly account for his gestures...' This activity has a favourable effect not only on the etheric body and its firmness, but also on controlling the etheric body by the astral body.

Artistic work on the gesture means to develop a feeling for the gesture that lives in speech, in this case, and it means to penetrate one's own gestures by self-awareness. This leads in a new way towards enhanced self-knowledge through new gestures that are formed by the ego. This may have an ordering, cleansing effect. So we can alter old acquired and encrusted habits by accompanying them with new movements and gestures.

I am speaking about gestures and movements that are made in connection with our breathing, that are carried on our breath, i.e. penetrated by our ego, and not of those that come voluntarily, impulsively or that are hard gestures controlled by the head. In our speech we have a sound gesture, a word gesture, a sentence gesture and a basic gesture. Especially in the last one 'we can clearly see that man can bring out his innermost experiences to the greatest effect only if he is able to let it flow right down into the movement of his hands. The human expression of gesture lives in the lifestream of the soul, which reaches as far as his hands and receives its visible expression in them. From there gesture reflects back on speech so that it becomes audible in speech.' (Christa Slezak-Schindler, *Der Schulungsweg der Sprachgestaltung*, Dornach 1994, S.58.)

Rudolf Steiner introduces six basic gestures of speech that were cultivated by the ancient Greeks in their mysteries as the six nuances of speech formation. These gestures are practised in movements and sentences which do not belong to any national language. They are original movements that are behind the language and that arise out of a spiritual region in which there is no definition of national languages.

Apart from these six revelations of speech there are no others. We hardly ever find them in pure gesture but always mixed in endless variations and possibilities of expression.

> And if we want to raise our speaking to consciousness, we should try to study how these shades of feelings come to expression in speech. It will, however, answer our purpose best if we do not at once proceed to a study of the spoken word, but first prepare the ground by a study of gesture, and then afterwards link the word onto the gesture. Proceeding in this way, we shall acquire a right feeling for the forming of speech, whereas by the reverse method, conclusions of an arbitrary nature would be constantly sug-

gesting themselves. Supposing, I mean, we were to start with the word (where the gesture has by now disappeared from view), with the idea of passing on thence to gesture. If, however, having recognized that the genius of speech works in these six ways, we then go on to study this genius of speech in gesture, we shall find that the way lies clear before us to go back afterwards to the word.
(Rudolf Steiner, *Speech and Drama*, London/New York, 1960, p. 55.)

The six basic gestures are:

Language expression	Gesture	Quality of voice
1. Effective	Pointing	Incisive
2. Thoughtful	Holding onto oneself	Full-toned
3. Feeling forwards against resistance or questioning	Rolling forward movement of arms and hands	Wavering, trembling
4. Antipathy	Flinging the limbs away from the body	Hard
5. Sympathy	Reaching out to touch	Soft
6. Withdrawing (onto one's own ground)	Slanting away of arms and hands from the body	Abrupt

In the following I shall try to show some ways of working with the six basic gestures on the different Doubles with respect to the four ether qualities.

If we think of the problem of Doubles that live in the warmth ether we can see that everything is related to the ego. It is however pretending to be an ego and has a strong need for recognition, and is looking for a personality to take the place of the ego, like for example a guru. In this case there is no proper self-awareness and one sways between feelings of inferiority or superiority. Practising the sixth basic gesture could be a help for finding a new balance in the one-sidedness of egocentricity. *Withdrawing* is a gesture that demands a strong, quiet and peaceful sphere and an awareness of uprightness—an acceptance of oneself—the way one is at a given time.

In order to feel the genuine situation a second basic gesture is helpful. *Thoughtfulness* brings back peace and quiet, and can deepen the situation in which we find ourselves. Speech becomes more full with this gesture and may resound with the wisdom we have been able to achieve.

One last gesture may help to overcome one's problem: this is the third, the *questioning gesture*. When asking a true question I must have the courage to open myself towards my environment. I admit that I do not know everything but that is no reason to think I value less because of that.

If we now turn to the problem of the Doubles living in the light ether and air, then we find ourselves between the danger of confusing associations that arise from too much light and the danger of drying out and hardening of thought by too much air.

In the first case practising the *gesture of antipathy*, which implies distance, clarity and firmness, can calm a quick, confusing association of thoughts and can create space for a true summing up of the situation. In the second case the *thoughtful gesture*, which is full of warmth and wisdom, can melt the harshness of thoughts.

And also in this the *gesture of withdrawal*, which calls for a strong presence of mind and true self-awareness in the present situation, is a good help for transforming those tendencies that induce us to live in a dream-world.

The Double living in the chemical ether develops apathy—a kind of indifference—that is caused by a too strong, almost 'watery' emotional life. This can be transformed by the *gesture of sympathy*. If directed towards the outside this gesture demands an interest in and openness towards one's environment and will motivate us.

If in life one is torn too much by emotions and moods, the *gesture of antipathy* with its distancing, slightly cold and clear movement is a good way to regain self-control.

In order to escape the dullness that is caused by tedious habits, or mechanical, disinterested automatism which seems overpowering, one can first start practising the *questioning gesture*. If performed in a genuinely questioning mood it can be a gentle help to regain interest and go back to the stream of life. Then, to intensify this process, one can practise the *gesture of effectiveness*. This gesture has a strong power that is directed towards the outside—by performing it one can convince others that the world is interesting.

When we come to the last ether, life ether, we meet with a Double that is deeply involved in power problems and relies on centralism in order to enforce his personal power. Here practising the sixth basic gesture, the *gesture of withdrawal*, is a chance to experience uprightness and self-centredness. On the other hand the *gesture of sympathy* is a strong means to transform the power of self-destruction in which this Double lives very strongly at times. And again the *gestures of sympathy and antipathy* towards oneself and towards the world facing us, as well as the *thoughtful gesture*, with its inner richness and warmth, are good means to become aware of oneself. This Double has the task of developing a new relationship towards the environment that is not based on power, control or violence. The *questioning gesture* calls for honest dedication and opening oneself towards the other person and can therefore be a first step in this direction.

These elements and interrelationships have slowly emerged

in my work with speech formation and learning from destiny and they should serve as an encouragement for further research in this wide and important field.

Awakening the Will
Principles and Processes in Adult Learning
Coenraad van Houten

How do adults learn? What is the task of the adult educator in adult education? What can adults do to take charge of their learning process?

Learning means change and transformation. But in order to learn, argues Coenraad van Houten, we must first awaken our will. True adult education, he says, enables our spritual ego to accomplish this. He describes the forms in which learning can be meaningfully structured, and offers advice and ideas to overcome specific learning blockages.

This book regards the business of adult education as a full profession, and it provides a theoretical and practical basis for its true task: an awakening of the will.

240 pp; 21.5 x 13.5 cm; paperback; £11.95; ISBN: 1 902636 21 X

Practising Destiny
Principles and Processes in Adult Learning
Coenraad van Houten
translated by J. Collis

More and more people are beginning to realize that education needs to continue throughout life. As individuals and collectively, we face the choice of either staying as we are, or striving constantly to develop.

Over decades of seminars and training work, Coenraad van Houten has developed three paths of learning for adults, each involving its own distinct method: 'Vocational Learning', 'Destiny Learning', and 'Spiritual Research Learning'. Although quite separate, the three paths are closely linked, with each building on the previous one.

This book depicts the sevenfold path of Destiny Learning. It is a path that leads through working in groups to a practical knowledge of karma. In addition, the seven professional fields of the adult educator are developed and described as an aid to self-training.

240 pp; 21.5 x 13.5 cm; paperback; £11.95; ISBN: 1 902636 21 X